To the Rescue

A book about God's rescue of His children

By Laurie Donahue

Illustrated by Ed Olson

Somis, CA

ISBN: 978-0-9799116-6-8

Published by LifeSong Publishers
P.O. Box 183, Somis, CA 93066-0183
805-504-3916
www.lifesongpublishers.com

Text by Laurie Donahue
www.LaurieDonahue.com

Illustrations by Ed Olson
www.designloftstudio.com

Thank you, Nicole Chin and Michael Regn for your editorial expertise.

Library of Congress Cataloging-in-Publication Data

Donahue, Laurie.
  To the rescue / by Laurie Donahue ; illustrated by Ed Olson.
    pages cm
  ISBN 978-0-9799116-6-8 (hardcover)
  1. Bible stories, English. 2. Children's poetry, American. I. Title.
  BS559.D66 2015
  220.95'05--dc23
                            2014032560

Look Up These Stories of Rescue

God's rescue of Noah and his family
Genesis 6:9-8:19

God's rescue of Moses and the Israelites from Egypt
Exodus 5:1-6:8 and Exodus 14:1-14:31

God's rescue of Jonah and the people of Ninevah
Jonah 1:1-3:3a

God's rescue of Shadrach, Meshach and Abednego in the fiery furnace
Daniel 3:8-3:30

God's rescue of Daniel in the lion's den
Daniel 6:1-6:28

God's rescue of Peter when he took his eyes off of Jesus
Matthew 14:22-14:33

God's rescue of Paul and Silas when they were in jail
Acts 16:16-16:39

Our Rescue:
Ephesians 2:1-10

Timeline
(not to scale)

A Word From Joni Eareckson Tada:

"With clever illustrations, and even wittier words, **To The Rescue** is a book adults will love reading to the children in their lives. What a great way to pique a child's interest in stories of the Bible which highlight God as a rescuer and deliverer... and what a smart way to help a child understand his own need to be rescued by the Lord! I happily recommend this unique publication to every parent who wishes to instill in his child an allure for the Word of God!"

—Joni Eareckson Tada, Joni and Friends International Disability Center

To Owen and Corban:

"May you know and trust the best Rescuer ever."
Grandma Laurie

To Linda:

"For all your support and encouragement!"
Ed

Save, rescue, free
His children big and small.
Worthy words woven,
Recorded for us all.

Rain, pour, flood
The waters didn't stop.
Bears, birds, bugs,
Things that walk and crawl and hop.

Save, rescue, free
His children big and small.
Even in a flood
And that's not all.

Waves, wet, cold
And Jonah's tossed in.
Run from God
A bad move for him.

Fire, sparks, hot
It's cooking up in there.
Three simple men
With nothing to fear,

Full of trust,
March past the oven door.
Eyes on God,
And now there's four.

Save, rescue, free
His children big and small.
God joined them
And that's not all!

Night, wind, fear,
Soles of feet are wet.
"Walk on water,
Come to Me, don't fret."

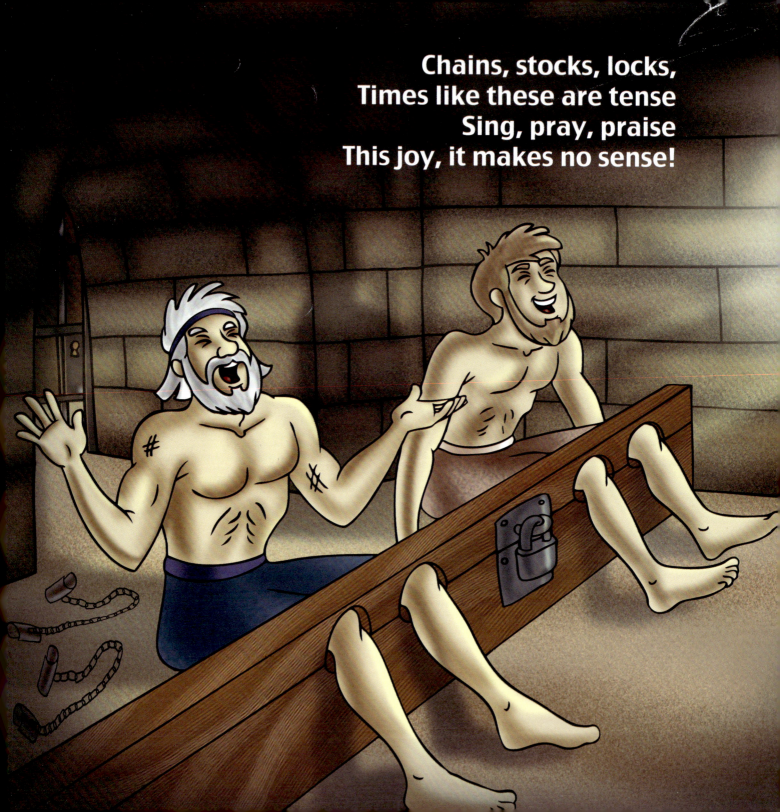

Self, idols, sin
I walked on my own path.
Blind, lifeless, lost
Heading for the cliff.

Love, call, save,
It's Jesus to the rescue.
Believe and receive
He made my heart brand new.

Save, rescue, free
Children one to ninety-four.
Trust Him today
And there isn't any more.

Laurie Donahue is a writer and occasional conference speaker living in Southern California. She has written or co-written six children's books and produced the 4-Ever His! music cd. Laurie has traveled on international medical mission trips with her husband to Uganda, Indonesia, Guatemala, and Mexico. Laurie desires to help children learn about things that really matter in a way that matters to them. You can learn more about her and read her blog at LaurieDonahue.com

Ed Olson is an illustrator and an animation artist/director who has worked with such companies as Walt Disney Animation, Warner Bros., Sony and Sega. His website is www.designloftstudio.com

The Bible is full of themes which begin in Genesis, the first book of the Bible, and course through to the end of Revelation, the last book. To the Rescue is the first book in my Themes of the Bible Series. This book contains only a few of the many examples of God's rescue of His children in Scripture. I am sure you can find many more examples in the Bible. I challenge you to look for them, and as you find them, go to www.LaurieDonahue.com/blog and leave a comment describing the example you found. Other readers will learn from you, as well. While you are there, please sign up for my blog and keep in touch with me. I look forward to hearing from you!

Laurie

Other Children's Books From
LifeSong Publishers

God... Should I Be Baptized?
by Laurie Donahue and Ralph Rittenhouse
(workbook for 8-12 years of age)

The Lord's Supper... Let's Get Ready!
by Laurie Donahue and Paul Phillipps
(workbook for 8-12 years of age)

Help Me Remember the Days of Creation
by Delphine Bates

Help Me Remember the Plagues of Egypt
by Delphine Bates

Help Me Remember the Ten Commandments
by Delphine Bates

Mr. Blue—A Job For You
by Laurie Donahue and Bryan Hintz
(with cut-out pieces for puzzle and play)

Find these plus Bible Studies and other books for adults at:
www.LifeSongPublishers.com
(or your favorite bookstore)
805-504-3916

He brought me out into a spacious place;
He rescued me because he delighted in me.
Psalm 18:19